The Mourning After

Hanna Haddad

BookLeaf Publishing

Presentation by *BookLeaf Publishing*

Web: www.bookleafpub.com

E-mail: info@bookleafpub.com

ISBN: 9789357690379

First edition 2023

Dedicated to my one and only sister, Maggie Haddad, who left us with irreparable broken hearts.

ACKNOWLEDGEMENT

To my parents and my brother, who have all had to endure the same sadness I have.

PREFACE

I lost my beautiful sister ten years ago, where one day she went to sleep and never woke up again.

This book is a compilation of poems depicting the sadness and struggles over the last ten years, living with the mourning after death.

SECONDS

It's been
Ten years,
Three months,
Two weeks,
Four days,
Six hours,
Fourteen minutes,
And there's not a second I don't miss you.

WORDS

I once told you I couldn't live without you.

You could've just taken my word.

FADED MEMORIES

Sometimes, I struggle to remember what life was like with you.

But I'm always reminded of what it's like without you.

SADNESS

I've never felt a sadness or loneliness like the day you died.

Except for every day since.

SOLACE

There's always tomorrow.

And that's what bothers me.

The only solace I get from living forever without
you,

Is knowing that I won't live forever.

RESENTMENT

I resent two things.

Seeing everyone who got to live except you.

Seeing everyone who gets to live except me.

KEEPING SCORE

But at the start I wasn't really sure,
Just who'd miss who more,
I wasn't sure how this all worked,
Or if I was the only one who'd hurt,
For it's something everyone knows,
It's always easier for the one that goes,
Than it is for those left behind,
You're only present in my mind,
And in the pieces of my broken soul,
I've spiralled out of control,
And the last ten years are blurred,
I don't remember much of what's occurred,
And this might sound a little extreme,
But sometimes I wonder if you only existed in
my dreams,
It's hard to believe you were ever really here,
But I guess the evidence is clear,
I don't really have to look too far,
Everything I do, there you are,
You've never escaped my mind,
But I'm the one left behind,
And you're free to fly wherever you like,
Like a bird who doesn't know wrong from right,
They only know the day from the night,
I always wonder what it's like for you,

Wonder if you miss us like we do,
Or maybe I'm just a little naïve,
And it's only what I want to believe,
And I once told you I couldn't live without you,
But you made me have to,
I don't really know how I've survived,
But my heart still beats without being alive,
But I doubt it's this hard for you,
You've already died, but I guess I have too,
So even though I haven't really been keeping
score,
I'm certain that I miss you, so much more.

REASONING

The biggest reason I'm still here,

Is not wanting to do to anyone else, what losing you has done to me.

STILL ALIVE

I'm scared to try new things,
Like smile and mean it.

No one grieves for the living,
But they should.

I died on the same day you did,
But they didn't give me a certificate.
They think I'm still alive,
Maybe technically,
But I can assure you, I've already died.

UNEVEN

"Happiness and sadness do not cancel each other out.
They live simultaneously alongside each other."

It's true. They do.

They're just really uneven.

LUCKY

Sometimes, people make me feel like I should
be moved on by now.

It's because they don't understand.

How lucky it is to be them.

DIFFERENCES

I was promised time would make it easier,

But it's only made it different.

I'm always scared that I'll lose someone else,

I'm not ready to do this again.

ONE THING

I only want one of two things to happen in this world.

For me to be truly happy.

Or for you to return.

Either one will do.
Because one isn't possible without the other,
But neither is possible at all.

WITHOUT YOU

Living without you,
I can still see beauty in life,
I can still see happiness around,
I can still see good in the world,
I can still see all these things.

But if I'm living without you,
I don't wish to enjoy any of them.

SUBSTANCE

I'd rather have sadness with substance,

Than happiness without.

The hardest part of losing you,

Was losing myself too.

CHOICES

People tell me that happiness is a choice.

But I can't possibly choose to be happy in the absence of your presence.

ALONE

Sometimes when I'm alone,
I call myself from your phone,
Hoping I'll hear your voice on the line,
But the only voice I hear is mine,
And you can't hear what I say but I don't care,
I still talk as though you're there,
And I tell you that I miss you too much,
And that eighteen years just wasn't enough,
And I tell you of the pain I've kept,
Of how you died, while I slept,
And I didn't even notice until it was too late,
And now all I could do was wait,
And I knew there was nothing more I could do,
But I still pumped your chest, 400 times like
they told me to,
And as you opened your eyes I still had hope,
All the while thinking that without you I can't
cope,
So they rushed over with sirens and lights,
To save the pretty young girl who had died
through the night,
But they came and said there was nothing we
could do,
As I felt my heart break in two,
So now when I call you it's only one way,

But I still have so much to say,
Like how much I love you,
And there's nothing I wouldn't do,
Just to hear you say,
I love you too.

YEARS

I don't celebrate people's birthdays anymore.

It's one less year we'll have them for.

WONDER

When I'm not enjoying something, I wonder,
how much longer do I have left of this.

But if I am enjoying something, I wonder the
same thing.

FOR GOOD

Our hearts don't break often.

They break once.

And they break for good.

TOO FAR GONE

But what will become of us?
Nothing.
We're too far gone.
Been here far too long,
That now it's comfortable,
I'm getting vulnerable,
But this is all we know,
Ten years and nothing to show,
Except a tally of regret,
We're as sad as sad can get,
Tracing around a silhouette,
Of before we became like this,
Before it hurt to reminisce,
Before time dissipated,
Before we were jaded,
Before life faded,
Before we hated,
I remember a time when we waited,
For the rest of our lives to start,
Now we're just falling apart,
And we carry around our broken hearts,
I keep mine in the top pocket of my shirt,
It's where I disguise all the hurt,
Because people think they can still hear it beat,
They still think it sounds complete,
They don't know I had to piece it back together,
From that time that it broke forever,

And I'm sure I left a few pieces on the floor,
Who cares, I don't really need them anymore,
I only keep them for decoration,
To avoid awkward conversation,
And after all my evaluations,
I'm merely waiting in anticipation,
For the day it finally gives in,
For when darkness finally wins,
And the pieces don't try to beat anymore,
Not like they did before,
And time can finally stop,
The pieces can forever drop,
And we can finally close the curtain,
But it only passes the burden,
And maybe it's no longer my concern,
Now that it's someone else's turn,
But what will become of them,
I can't even remember when,
Exactly I crossed the line,
To too far gone from doing fine,
It's like it happened overnight,
Like it didn't even put up a fight,
Just packed its bags for a first class flight,
Kissed everyone goodbye, said I'm going too far,
Now they just sit, and they wait, asking what
will become of him.
Nothing.
He's too far gone.